Original title:
Coral Reef Voices

Copyright © 2025 Creative Arts Management OÜ
All rights reserved.

Author: Christian Leclair
ISBN HARDBACK: 978-1-80587-410-2
ISBN PAPERBACK: 978-1-80587-880-3

The Illuminated Abyss

Down in the deep, where the fish like to dance,
An octopus waves in a glittery trance.
He juggles with shells and throws colorful beads,
While the clownfish snicker, as laughter precedes.

A crab plays the drums with his pincers of flair,
Seahorses groove, swinging here and there.
A parrotfish grins, with a toothy delight,
Singing underwater, they party all night.

Ballads of the Tidepools

In tidepools so bright, all the critters convene,
A starfish recites, like a fishy machine.
The hermit crab hums with a shell on his back,
While slugs take a bow, dressed in jackets of black.

The seaweed waves sweetly, it's part of the band,
As sea urchins bounce, taking turns on the sand.
With laughter and giggles, they sit side by side,
Singing their songs with unbridled pride.

Euphony of the Eddies

In the swirl of the eddies, the fish form a line,
They do a quick shuffle, it's truly divine!
With bubbles and giggles, they swirl all around,
While the snails take a break, in their shells they are drowned.

A bobtail squid grins, adds a splash of surreal,
As bass sing a chorus, that's part of the reel.
The blowfish puffs out, tries not to look shy,
While a grouper just rolls his big googly eye.

The Splash of the Unknown

In waters so bright, something funny appears,
A fish with a hat and a giggle of cheers.
With a wink and a wiggle, he joins in the fun,
While the turtles all chuckle, "Our day's just begun!"

A dolphin's loud laughter fills up the wide sea,
As sea cucumbers sway, it's a sight to see!
With each dive and splash, they embrace the surprise,
In this watery world, let the humor arise!

Underwater Serenade

Bubbles rise like ticklish giggles,
Fish waltz while the seaweed wriggles.
Crabs do a shuffle, clumsy and bold,
They dance like they've got treasures of gold.

Starfish chill with a laid-back grin,
Sea cucumbers join it, they're in for the win.
A clam shows off its shiny shell,
In this underwater circus, all is swell.

Symphony of the Sea

Octopus plays the drums with flair,
Clownfish laugh without any care.
Dolphins leap with glee in a line,
While sea turtles think they're divine.

This orchestra feels like a grand parade,
With jellyfish twirling, like a serenade.
The sea sounds playful, a bubbly delight,
Underwater sounds that tickle the night.

Dances of the Anemones

Wiggly wonders in a colorful bloom,
Anemones twirl with a funky zoom.
A shrimp gets caught in their wiggly sway,
He jokes, "I'm just here for a buffet!"

They bounce and they jiggle, a joyful spree,
While the little fish giggle, "Look at me!"
In this ocean party, so quirky and bright,
Every voice drums up a giggle tonight.

Ocean's Harmonious Murmur

Whales hum ballads from deep down below,
While seahorses sway with a vibrant flow.
A parrotfish shouts, 'I'm the best singer!',
But all the sea critters just think he's a stinger!

With coral polka dots, they dance about,
Making silly faces and laughing out loud.
The tide brings in laughter, oh what a sight,
Underwater echoes, pure joy and delight!

Ode to the Ocean's Beauty

Bubbles pop like champagne corks,
Under the sea, where time just forks.
Fish in tuxedos doing their dance,
Anemones swaying, what a romance!

Starfish lounging without a care,
Crabs in top hats, a real debonair.
Seashells gossiping, oh what a scene,
The ocean's a party, you're unseen!

The Secrets That Live Beneath

Whispers of fish in shades of bright,
Worrying over what to wear tonight.
Octopuses playing hide-and-seek,
Turtles taking selfies; oh, so unique!

A choir of clams with a shellfish tune,
Bubble-blowers dancing under the moon.
Secrets of mermaids tucked in their scales,
Plotting their pranks as the dolphin wails!

Whispers of the Wave Whisperers

Wave riders giggle as they crash,
Surfboards made of jelly, oh, what a splash!
Seagulls squawk like a comedy show,
While sea cucumbers steal the show!

Barnacles gossip about the tide,
Urchins snicker, nowhere to hide.
Shells conspire, they plot and scheme,
Life's a stage, it's all just a dream!

Echoing Through the Fishbowl

Goldfish prancing, they flash with glee,
While guppies gossip like it's high tea.
The water's a wonder, a funny affair,
When bubbles escape through a non-existent chair!

Betta fish flaunt with flair and pride,
Scoffing at each other, in fancies they glide.
Echoes of laughter ripple along,
In the fishbowl's world, we all belong!

Beneath the Waters' Whisper

Bubbles rise in silly loops,
Fish parade in tiny groups.
A turtle grins, what a sight,
Winking tales in morning light.

Seaweed sways, it's got the moves,
An octopus makes all the groves.
With sea cucumbers in a line,
Doing the cha-cha, oh so fine!

Shrimp are gossiping, oh dear,
About the starfish sipping beer.
A crab decided he would dance,
He stumbled twice, now isn't that a chance?

In the depths where giggles seep,
Anemones tickle in their sleep.
Chasing bubbles with delight,
Laughter echoes, what a sight!

A Journey Through the Blue

In the blue where the fish play,
Starfish giggle, 'What a day!'
A dolphin pops up, full of zest,
'Time for a race, who's the best?'

Seahorses sway, with tiny tunes,
Dancing 'neath the shining moons.
A clownfish laughs, so very bright,
Tickled by a jelly - what a fright!

Bubbles bounce like jumpy beans,
While whales play tag in silver sheens.
The sea's a stage, come take a look,
With mermaids giving all the hooks!

Turtles trying to break dance,
Flipping, flopping, not by chance.
In this blue, where fun won't end,
Every wave's a happy friend!

Tides of Enchantment

Waves giggle as they crash and curl,
The sea stars shine in a twinkly swirl.
A fish wearing glasses, oh what a pair,
Says 'Ready for a show? Come grab a chair!'

The clams are whispering, tales so tall,
Of grand adventures and seafoam brawls.
A sea urchin tells a punny joke,
While crabs crack up and start to croak.

Underwater, where secrets lie,
A narwhal sings with a dreamy sigh.
He juggles pearls like a circus pro,
While tiny shrimp watch the grand show.

The rhythm sways, the mermaids cheer,
As sea turtles glide with no fear.
In this tide of laughter and glee,
What a splash—come swim with me!

The Pulse of the Ocean

In the ocean's heart, laughter flows,
With every pulse, the mischief grows.
A fish in a bow tie tells a tale,
Of swimming races in a festive gale.

An octopus plays chess with a crab,
Both of them decked out, what a fab!
A conch shell's squeak makes everyone stop,
'Join my conga line, hop, hop, hop!'

Coral castles echo with delight,
As sea turtles dine on seaweed bites.
Dolphins wear shades, oh so neat,
Sipping seawater, a fine treat!

As the tide tickles all that was,
The ocean whispers; it's just because.
Joy dances where waves sway wide,
In this realm, let the fun be your guide!

Voices in the Brine

In the depths where bubbles play,
Fish dance in a wacky sway.
An octopus with juggling hands,
Serves up laughs across the sands.

Clams clap their shells in a merry beat,
While seahorses two-step on their tiny feet.
A pufferfish with a giggle so loud,
Turns the blue into a bubbly crowd.

Starfish tell tales with a wiggly twist,
Of pirate ships and a treasure missed.
Jellyfish float with a squishy grace,
Waving hello with a gelatinous face.

Oh, beneath the waves, the humor thrives,
As fishy friends share their funny lives.
Together they make the ocean boom,
With laughter that can light up any room.

Chronicles of the Churning Waters

In swirling currents, stories unfold,
A clownfish tumbles, always bold.
A crab in a hat, oh what a sight,
Challenges a shark to a tickle fight.

Anemones giggle as they sway,
While snails sneak up, slow and gray.
The fish gossip with shimmery scales,
About the mischief of the crabby tales.

With bubbles bursting, secrets shared,
An old sea turtle, though slightly scared,
Tells a joke with a wink and a grin,
That makes all the little fish spin.

Oh, in these waters, the laughter's loud,
As friends celebrate, an ocean crowd.
The waves their stage, the sea their muse,
In this salty world, we can't refuse.

Melodies of the Multicolored

From vibrant hues of red and blue,
Comes a fish with a kazoo!
It toots a tune that makes them dance,
As bubbles float in a frothy trance.

A hermit crab plays a tiny drum,
While sea turtles sway, oh so numb.
They band together, forming a choir,
Singing sea shanties, never to tire.

There's laughter in the wriggly sway,
As jellyfish blind us with their display.
Their luminescent glow, a light show grand,
While mermaids giggle, hand in hand.

In this colorful world, we find our cheer,
A symphony of joy, crystal clear.
With a splash and a giggle, they float away,
Transforming the ocean into a cabaret.

Tranquil Tales from the Tides

On soft waves where the sea stars gleam,
A dolphin grins, in silly dream.
Telling stories wrapped in delight,
As rays of sun turn dark to bright.

A seagull swoops with a cheeky call,
Cracking jokes, the best of all.
While plankton twirl in a dizzy dance,
Embracing life's playful chance.

The wisdom of oysters adds to the fun,
While fish flip-flop in the sun.
Each wave whispers tales of mirth,
Of joyful days and ocean's worth.

In tranquil tides where laughter roams,
The sea is alive; it feels like home.
With giggles echoing, carrying high,
In this watery realm, the spirits fly.

Reflections of the Abyss

A fish with a hat swam by with a grin,
He said, 'It's too bright! I'll never fit in!'
With bubbles of laughter, they danced in delight,
Twirling and swirling with all of their might.

A clam spat a pearl—precious and round,
'It's perfect for pondering this silly sound!'
Starfish laughed loudly, a real clown in view,
Saying, 'I can't clap, but I'll still join the crew!'

An octopus juggled some seaweed with pride,
'Not bad for a guy who's got eight arms to guide!'
They snicker and chuckle, what a merry scene,
Ocean's finest jesters, so silly, so keen!

With friends all around, not a worry in sight,
They laughed till they bubbled, oh, what pure delight!
In the depths of the blue, where joy never ceased,
You'll find all the critters enjoying their feast.

Tidal Echoes

A jellyfish bounced on a wave of pure glee,
'Look at me, look at me, I'm floating so free!'
Crabs passed by clicking their claws in a dance,
Said one with a wink, 'It's a crustacean chance!'

A dolphin popped up, with a splash and a spin,
'Why swim in circles when we can all begin?'
Seahorses giggled, tied knots in their tails,
'It's tough to be serious when tickled by whales!'

A school of bright fish sang tunes of the sea,
'We're the scales of laughter, won't you swim with me?'
With bubbles like music, they twirled and they swayed,
Making ocean memories in this grand escapade!

At twilight's soft whisper, they all gathered 'round,
Swapping fishy tales with a joyous sound!
And as the moon shone on this watery floor,
The tides echoed laughter from the deep and the shore.

The Ocean's Rhapsody

A crab with a kazoo led a band of bright fish,
'Come join us for tunes—this could be your wish!'
With turtles on tambourines, shining and bright,
They rocked and they rolled in the soft ocean light.

A pufferfish puffed up to chime in the beat,
'No one plays better when you're full of sweet treat!'
The chorus of barnacles joined with a cheer,
'We'll see you at the concert, the big show is near!'

With seaweed confetti floating down from the sky,
A seagull swooped low, gave a great big goodbye.
The dolphins were diving, the sea stars would sway,
Creating a symphony of fun every day!

And as sunset painted the waves all aglow,
The laughter of ocean life began to flow.
With each wave that crashed, joy rang out like a song,
In this splashy wonderland, where all friends belong.

Driftwood Ballads

A driftwood guitar played by a cheeky fish,
'Let's get together, it's a watery wish!'
With the sound of the tides, they danced on the sand,
A crab played the disco, oh wasn't it grand?

A sea cucumber twirled, in a stunning ballet,
'Watch me unfold like a bright ocean ray!'
Jellyfish floated by in their silken best dress,
'We're here for the party, you can guess the rest!'

A flounder brought cookies, shaped like the sea,
'One bite and you'll see how silly we can be!'
Mermaids all giggled, with hair made of foam,
'I hear the tunes calling, let's dance to our home!'

As the moonlight sparkled on this festive shore,
A chorus erupted—'We want even more!'
With laughter and rhythm, hearts swollen with joy,
The ocean embraced them, every girl and boy!

Harmonies in Hues

In bright blue waters, fish do dance,
They wiggle and giggle, taking a chance.
With fins a-flutter and tails a-swish,
They gossip and chuckle, oh what a swish!

A turtle grins wide, as he floats by,
"Did you hear the joke about the sly guy?"
He cracks up the clams, the seaweeds all laugh,
As the old octopus crafts a funny graph.

Anemones sway, with ticklish delight,
"Hey sea cucumbers, you're quite a sight!"
They juggle some shells, they juggle some sand,
These silly sea creatures, life's just so grand!

With colors ablaze, like a painter's delight,
They sing underwater, from morning till night.
Each bubble a giggle, each wave a fresh jest,
In this aquatic realm, they're simply the best!

The Siren's Song

Down in the depths, a siren sings loud,
Her voice makes the fish all gather around.
"Why did the seahorse cross the big blue?
To ask the clownfish for tips on his hue!"

Octopus giggles, while tying a shoe,
"Can you tie mine too? I've got quite the crew!"
Starfish flip-flop, all out of time,
"Can someone explain this dance to my rhyme?"

A dolphin appears, with a splash and a roll,
"My flips are the best, they're the life of the shoal!"
The seagull above, mutters, "Oh what a joke!
Can I join this circus, where laughter's bespoke?"

With melodies bubbling, the ocean's alive,
Each creature a bard, together they thrive.
In waves of nice humor, their laughter grows strong,
As they share all their secrets in the siren's song!

Whims of the Watery World

A pufferfish jokes, "I'm not just a sight!
I'm also a chef, see my cooking tonight!"
With seaweed casserole, he serves up a plate,
But watch out for spikes, they might ruin your fate!

The crabs are all chatting, with claws in the air,
"Did you hear 'bout the clam? He's got quite a flair!"
They tap their own shells to keep up the beat,
And show off their moves with eight-legged heat.

A narwhal struts in, "I'm the unicorn here!
My horn is a gift, and it's quite full of cheer."
They all share a laugh at the gags of the sea,
In the ever-blue waters, it's a sight to see!

With bubbles a-bursting and laughter that swirls,
The whims of this world bring joy to the twirls.
In every wave's crash, their spirits take flight,
With each tickle of tide, they revel in light!

Enchantments in Aquamarine

Beneath the blue surface where laughter ignites,
The sea creatures gather for oceanic nights.
A crab in a tux, says, "Watch my grand dance!"
As he twirls and he spins, giving all a good chance.

A blowfish declares, "Look how puffed I can be!
I'm serious—watch how much fun it can be!"
With colors like rainbows, he wiggles about,
Making fish friends giggle and shout, "What's that about?"

The jellyfish float, with their whims so divine,
They glow in the dark, "Let's play glow-in-the-line!"
While mantas and eels zoom on by with delight,
Creating a show that's a marvelous sight!

In aquamarine dreams, where joy never fades,
The sea sings in chorus, in shimmering shades.
With silly adventures, they weave through the heaves,
In this magical realm, it's joy that retrieves!

The Murmuration of Marine Mysteries

In the blue, a fish does twirl,
With a flick of fins, they swirl.
"Hey, watch me do the cha-cha!"
Said a clownfish, full of drama.

Nudibranchs wear colors bright,
Jellyfish float, what a sight!
"Is it my turn to lead?" asks one,
While crabs argue over who's most fun.

A sea turtle chimes in glee,
"I'm slow and steady, can't you see?"
But a shrimp darts past, so fast,
Saying, "Catch me if you dare, you big, old blast!"

Under waves where laughter gleams,
With bubbles rising, so it seems,
The ocean's party never sleeps,
As even starfish giggle in heaps.

The Underwater Ballet

In the depths, a dance begins,
Where octopuses wear their sins.
With arms that flail and twist just right,
They pirouette away from fright.

The sea cucumbers do their best,
While angelfish put them to the test.
"Who knew we'd have such flair?" they tease,
As they glide through currents with such ease.

A dolphin spins, a mermaid sighs,
"That's not ballet; it's just goodbyes!"
They splash and laugh, a grand display,
As the seaweeds sway and join the play.

With every bubble, every swirl,
The ocean floor becomes a whirl.
Together they twirl, what a sight,
Underwater dreams in pure delight.

Secrets in Sapphire

In the depths, tales are spun,
Where fish gossip just for fun.
"Did you hear about the kraken?"
"Oh please, that's just a bit of a crackin!"

Seahorses whisper in a shoal,
"Did you see that whirling whale's roll?"
They giggle softly, hold their breath,
While pondering tales of underwater theft.

Starfish grin with sarcastic charm,
"Who needs legs when you have such arms?"
And pufferfish puff in sheer delight,
Proving being round can feel just right.

In sapphire waves, secrets hide,
With every ebb, there's more inside.
From eel to plankton, all agree,
The ocean's a stage; come join the spree!

The Depths Sing

Down below where the light is dim,
The fish gather, and they all swim.
"Shall we harmonize?" says the bass,
As the sea anemone joins the class.

With each bubble, a note escapes,
As laughter follows, in silly shapes.
"Shhhh! That's our cue!" cries the old trout,
"Oh, it's just dolphins bullying about!"

Clownfish croon in funny tones,
While wrasses dance on coral bones.
"Take it down a notch!" the grouper pleads,
"It's more of a jam when no one reads!"

Yet in the depths, a chorus swells,
With every splash, the ocean tells,
That in this world beneath the sun,
It's the quirkiest tunes that win the fun.

Tales of the Ocean's Pulse

In the deep, where the fishes tease,
A clownfish giggles in the breeze.
The jellyfish wobbles with such grace,
While shrimp do the cha-cha, keeping pace.

An octopus, pranked with colors bright,
Changes hues, oh what a sight!
A starfish laughs, if only it could,
But all it can do is sit where it would.

A turtle spins tales, quite absurd,
Of seaweed dances and a quirky bird.
The crabs do the conga with a snap,
Underwater, there's never a dull gap.

The seahorses trot, in a line so neat,
Whispering secrets as they meet.
With giggles and bubbles all around,
In this ocean, laughter abounds.

Water's Choral Dance

Bubbles rise like giggles, oh so sweet,
While dolphins twist in a synchronized beat.
The fish start a choir, voices galore,
"Hooray for the ocean!" they loudly implore.

A clam joins in with a shell-ish song,
"Sing with me, everyone, come along!"
A starfish applauds with its waving arms,
"Join our fun, it's filled with charms!"

The sea anemone sways, all aflutter,
As the plankton wiggle, well, that's the butter!
A horde of squids decide to dance,
With ink-spilled laughter, they take a chance.

As waves clap their hands in delight,
Creatures all revel in this playful night.
With gurgles and giggles, let's not take a stance,
Together we'll join in this watery dance!

Rhapsody of the Briny

An anglerfish grins with a wink and a nod,
Chasing after a remora, oh what a fraud!
With prankster wit, they forge a delight,
As currents swirl, they dance through the night.

A puffer fish puffs, thinking it's bold,
Displaying the bravado of stories untold.
But it rolls away, oh what a sight,
In water world, it's more of a plight!

Glimmering shells gossip, oh what a show,
As sea cucumbers shuffle, moving slow.
The barnacles chatter, getting the scoop,
Of mermaids' secrets in their underwater loop.

In this soggy concert, we laugh and we cheer,
From whale songs deep to the tickles near.
The oceans, a symphony, quirky and vast,
Where humor and joy are forever meant to last!

Serenade Among the Seaweed

Seaweed sways like a dancer's gown,
Tickling the bottom with a comical frown.
A crab with a top hat struts in delight,
As sea urchins giggle at the funny sight.

Anemones wave to the fish passing by,
"Join our party!" they chirp with a sigh.
While snails slide down on a slimy slide,
Their laughter echoing with nowhere to hide.

The kelp forms a band, they're ready to play,
With a seahorse drummer tapping away.
"Let's sing a tune beneath the blue haze,
Of jellyfish jigs and mackerel ways!"

A turtle does backflips, oh such a flair,
While clownfish invite friends from everywhere.
Under the waves, where giggles take hold,
The melody of madness is joyfully bold!

Lullabies from the Abyss

In the ocean's cradle, fish do sing,
With bubbles and giggles, they dance and swing.
A starfish plays tambourine with glee,
While crabs play the trombone, wild and free.

The jellyfish float, with jelly-like flair,
In a disco of currents, without a care.
An octopus jokes, with eight arms in tow,
Making silly faces, putting on a show.

Clownfish chuckle, with stripes so bright,
They tickle the seaweed, oh, what a sight!
Turtles tell tales of the ones that got lost,
All while the sea otters juggle, at cost.

The sea cucumbers grunt, with a snore so loud,
As they nap in the sand, feeling quite proud.
Whales hum lullabies that drift through the night,
While dolphins play tag, in the moon's soft light.

Colors of the Tide

In waters so vivid, a hue-tastic spree,
A parrotfish laughs, painting coral with glee.
Blue, pink, and orange, a riotous cheer,
Each splash tells a joke for the fishlings to hear.

Yellow tangs gossip, but oh, what a source!
They wiggle and giggle, on a gossiping course.
With a wink and a wiggle, they race past the rocks,
Swapping the tales of the latest fish flocks.

The sea grass is waving, with green frisky tunes,
While the clownfish perform their old silly boons.
A lionfish darts with his spiky crown,
Claiming he's king, but he doesn't wear a gown.

The hermit crabs shuffle, in shells brightly worn,
Making faces at fish; oh, their antics adorn!
The vibrant sea floor, a playful parade,
In the ocean's bright carnival, laughter is made.

Voices of the Silent Depths

In deep water echoes, a grumpy old grouper,
Claims he's the wisest, an underwater trooper.
He grumbles and gripes, with a voice like a fog,
Yet he trips on his fins, like a clumsy old dog.

A sneak-thief shrimp, all dressed up for a show,
Steals pearls from the clams, puts on a sly glow.
He chuckles in rhythm, a trickster's delight,
As the seaweed giggles, in the pale moonlight.

A sea turtle declares, "I'm slow but I'm wise,"
While the puffers just snicker, rolling their eyes.
"We'll zoom past your shell, like a flash of bright scales,
While you drift in the calm, spinning seaweed trails!"

Yet down in the depths, the laughter resounds,
As creatures tell tales of the ocean's great bounds.
With whispers and chuckles, they swim through the dark,
Turning tides of laughter into a light-hearted spark.

The Beneath's Revelry

Beneath the blue skies, where the currents swirl,
The fish throw a party, giving fins a twirl.
With sea urchin hats, and bubbles for drinks,
They dance in the sand, causing giggles and winks.

Anemones sway, with a tickle and tease,
Enticing the clownfish to dance with great ease.
They bob up and down, in a syncopated spree,
As the shrimp keeps the rhythm, quite fancy and free.

A dolphin slides in, with a flip and a spin,
"Who needs a disco? Let the fun now begin!"
The stingrays glide by, in a graceful ballet,
While seahorses tango, in their quirky way.

The sea is a stage, with each creature a star,
Sharing tales of the depths, both near and far.
With laughter and joy, in the splash of the sea,
The depths hold a party, just waiting for thee!

Symphony of the Shallow Depths

In the depths where fish do prance,
A grouper winks, ready to dance.
Jellyfish float in a slow ballet,
"Don't sting me, please," a clownfish did say.

Starfish hold a family meeting,
With sea urchins, they're all competing.
An octopus plays hide and seek,
While shrimp crack jokes, with glee they squeak.

Anemones wave like they're on stage,
A parrotfish joins, it's all the rage.
With bubbles that tickle, and laughter around,
In the shallow depths, joy is profound!

Every creature has something to share,
Even crabs don't forget to beware.
With harmony swirling, it's quite a scene,
Underwater antics, oh what a dream!

Harmonious Spirits of the Sea

Down below where the seaweed sways,
A seahorse prances in quirky ways.
With a wink and a smile, he twirls with glee,
"Join my conga line, come dance with me!"

Dolphins burst forth in jokes and jests,
Competing in flips that are simply the best.
Turtles chuckle, all laid-back and chill,
While fish gossip close, they just can't keep still.

Shrimps are busy with their pranks and games,
While eels are telling the wildest claims.
In the ocean's rhythm, they all unite,
Creating laughter from morning to night.

A conch shell shouts, "Let's not be late!"
As the ocean sings, they celebrate.
What a symphony, bright and bold,
With spirits so free, the stories unfold!

Tales from the Water's Edge

At the water's edge where laughter lies,
A pelican drops in with a big surprise.
Crabs on the sand start to spin and twirl,
As egrets laugh, it's a feathery whirl.

The tide rolls in, and so do the jokes,
Oysters giggle at the clumsy strokes.
"Let's catch some sun!" said a silly fish,
"I'll wear a hat, that's my only wish!"

A parrot squawks with a gossip spree,
Telling tales of the jellyfish tea.
With shells as hats and seaweed ties,
They dance to the rhythm beneath the skies.

With waves of chuckles, and splashes loud,
Every critter feels merry and proud.
Tales of the tide, forever will last,
In the watery world, fun's unsurpassed!

The Murmur of Shells and Sand

On grains of sand where stories flow,
Seashells whisper tales, all aglow.
A beach ball floats, chased by a crab,
"Catch me if you can!" he gave a gab.

A sea turtle paddles with goofy grace,
While a dolphin shows off in a funny race.
Waves clap their hands, what a great cheer,
For the funny fish that swim near and dear!

With laughter echoing under the tide,
A playful sea star takes a wild ride.
While hermit crabs barter shells with flair,
"Your glittery pink for my worn-out chair?"

As the sunset glimmers on bubbly seas,
Fish share their jokes carried by the breeze.
In this soft murmur, joy finds its way,
In every splash and laugh, they play!

Beneath Whirling Waters

Bubbles giggle as fish swim by,
A turtle winks and gives a sigh.
Clownfish juggle with seaweed flair,
While shrimps breakdance without a care.

Starfish hold a talent show,
Each limb a gift, a quirky glow.
Octopus dazzles, a master of disguise,
In this swirling world, laughter flies.

Eels play hide and seek all day,
Puffers puff in a silly way.
The sea's a stage for giggly scenes,
Where every critter has their means.

In this playground of colors and sounds,
The joy of the ocean forever abounds.
With each splash, a chuckle is found,
A funny bounce in the sea's surround.

Murmurs from the Ocean's Heart

Whales gossip in waves of blue,
While rays get tangled in kelp that's new.
A crab with a hat sings a silly tune,
As seahorses waltz under the moon.

Jellyfish have a pulsing beat,
They groove while having a treat of seaweed sweet.
Fish tell tales of adventurous fun,
In a swirling dance, their work is done.

Sandy gulls squawk as if they know,
The secrets of tides in the ebb and flow.
With every splash, a cheeky jest,
In this vibrant world, who'd want to rest?

From the depths of the deep to the shimmering shore,
The ocean's laughter, we must explore.
In the rhythm of currents, joy can be found,
As the heart of the sea offers its sound.

Portraits in Turquoise

Fish flash like artists with bold strokes,
Each hue a prank, each wiggle evokes.
A puffin wearing a silly smile,
Poses for selfies, staying a while.

Gentle octo plans a grand parade,
With crabs in hats that never fade.
The sea anemone throws a ball,
Where every sea creature can have a sprawl.

Bright parrotfish paint the sea with glee,
While hermit crabs swap shells to see.
Fish don costumes and dance, oh so spry,
In this underwater life, joy is the why.

Every swirl of water is filled with cheer,
A portrait of laughter, always near.
In turquoise scenes, the funny unfolds,
As the canvas of life's wonder holds.

Currents of Memory

In currents where giggles flow like gold,
The tales of the sea creatures are bold.
A dolphin pranks with a misty spray,
As fish join together in humorous play.

Tides whisper stories of years gone by,
Of snail races that made everyone cry.
With bubbles as balloons, the fun is bright,
Under the waves, the laughter takes flight.

Squids sketch murals of goofy looks,
With stories that outshine the best of books.
The tides carry echoes of laughter so sweet,
In the ocean's embrace, every heart has a beat.

With each woosh of water, memories come alive,
In the depths of laughter, joy will thrive.
Currents of fun wrap the sea in delight,
As the ocean twinkles through day and night.

Secrets of the Submerged World

In the deep, where fish do prance,
A octopus wore a crazy pants.
He danced with glee, he spun with style,
While seahorses giggled all the while.

A crab with shades and fancy shoes,
Said, "I'm off to win the blues!"
He clapped his claws in perfect time,
While jellyfish jived to rhythm and rhyme.

The parrotfish wore a jaunty hat,
He scoffed at turtles, saying, "Look at that!"
They zoomed and zipped, with merry cheer,
Bubbles of laughter filled the sphere.

Among the hues that shimmer bright,
A clownfish joked, causing delight.
With every splash, a wave of glee,
In this hidden world, oh, how fun to be!

The Call of the Anemone

An anemone danced in the breeze,
Calling clowns, "Come join, if you please!"
With arms wide open, it swayed to the beat,
As fish lined up, ready for a treat.

"I'm the host with the most!" it cried,
While a starfish blushed, feeling snide.
Tentacles waving like a grand parade,
Creating a scene where laughter was made.

A shrimp chimed in, with jokes so grand,
"By my side, it's a fun land!"
While bubbles floated in sunny beams,
The friends all giggled, lost in dreams.

A party within the aquatic glow,
Where humor flows, and joy must grow.
In this anemone's vibrant show,
Laughter echoed, a beautiful flow!

Rhythm of the Reef's Heartbeat

Beneath the waves, a funky beat,
Fish flash-danced with rapid feet.
A trumpet-blowing fish led the way,
While doodlebugs swirled, ready to play.

Turtles bobbed, keeping in time,
To the bubble bop, a joyful rhyme.
Octopuses juggled with flair and fun,
As sunlight trickled—oh, what a run!

Crabs pranced proudly, strutting their stuff,
Cackling loudly, they just had enough!
A sea urchin grinned, doing the twist,
"Join in, my friends! You can't resist!"

With every splash, every flip and dive,
The reef came alive, what a thrilling hive!
In this dance of delight, they showed their art,
The rhythm of joy is a beating heart.

Serenade of the Sea Spheres

In the abyss of shimmering moons,
Creatures sing their playful tunes.
A whale hummed deep, a sweet serenade,
While shrimps tapped toes in their parade.

A flounder pranced with a silly grin,
"Join the fun, let the show begin!"
With bubbles popping like jolly balloons,
The underwater night was full of cartoons.

Stars twinkled bright, like confetti below,
As dolphins laughed, 'round they'd go.
"Tails up high!" the jellies cheered,
Creating a whirlpool of joy, not feared.

Each splash a note in this musical flair,
Each ocean sway a dance, so rare.
In the serendipity of the sea spheres,
Laughter echoed, silencing fears.

Aquatic Whispers

In the blue, the fish all chatter,
As a turtle rolls, they laugh and splatter.
A crab jives, a seahorse swings,
Silly jokes make the ocean sing.

A clam winks with a shell full of dreams,
While jellyfish float like whimsical beams.
A dolphin flips, does a backflip dance,
"Oh look," he chuckles, "I'm wearing pants!"

Octopus brings his eight-legged flair,
Telling tall tales of the deep sea air.
"Why did the fish blush?" he grins with glee,
"Because it saw the ocean's big knee!"

Through bubbles of laughter, the waters gleam,
Where sea creatures play, and everything's a dream.
With a splash and a giggle, they all unite,
In a dance that sparkles, oh what a sight!

Beneath the Floating Gardens

Beneath the waves, a garden's glee,
With fish that sing and dance so free.
A starfish poses like a movie star,
"Hey, check my moves, I'm going far!"

The anemones sway, in a gentle groove,
While clownfish joke, "Hey, make a move!"
With a pufferfish puffed up full of pride,
He shouts, "I'm the reason the sea's so wide!"

Shrimp in tuxedos tap dance in pairs,
As seaweed sways and the humor flares.
"Why don't fish play cards?" they laugh a lot,
"Because they're always getting caught!"

With bubbles of giggles drifting all around,
Among the laughter, joy is found.
Under the waves, life's a jolly spree,
In this funny world, just let it be!

The Depths' Gentle Lull

In the hush of the deep, where the sea stars yawn,
A sleepy shark sneaks past, thinking it's dawn.
With dreams of snacks, oh what a sight,
He naps on a reef, dreaming of bites.

Grouper is grumpy, with crusty old tales,
Of fishing trips gone wrong and sea-faring fails.
"But why is it funny?" a young fish inquires,
"Because we all live in a sea of liars!"

A wise old turtle joining the rest,
Says, "In the deep, it's really a jest.
Why did the crab never share his food?
Because he was feeling a bit too shrewd!"

So snooze in the depths, with laughs on the side,
Where ocean's lullabies awake the tide.
In this watery world, humor will stay,
As they dance through the night, in their playful play!

A Canvas of Undersea Colors

In splashes of colors, the ocean inspires,
With bright painted fish, their antics never tire.
A parrotfish giggles as it munches away,
"Graffiti on my scales? Who says I can't play?"

Squid scribbles lines in a swirling dance,
As clowns juggle pearls, in a shimmering trance.
"Why did the fish break up?" the grouper does tease,
"Because they couldn't find common seas!"

With hues of the rainbow, they play tag and spin,
While corals add flair, like a party within.
"Look at me!" shouts a tang, with a flip and a whirl,
"I'm the life of the ocean, I'm ready to twirl!"

Each shade tells a story, every wave makes us smile,
As laughter threads through every sea mile.
With a wink and a splash, joyfully they flow,
In this canvas of life, their colors aglow!

Whispers of the Ocean Floor

In the deep where the fishes twirl,
A clownfish tells jokes, gives a swirl.
"Why did the crab never share his snack?"
"He was a little shellfish, always on the attack!"

The sea urchins giggle, all pointy and proud,
"We prick you, don't poke us!" they say to the crowd.
A starfish chimes in with a wink and a grin,
"I'm just here chillin', let the laughter begin!"

An octopus juggles with flair and finesse,
While seahorses cheer, dressed up in a mess.
"Watch what you're doing with all of those arms!"
"I'm no octo-punster, but I sure got charms!"

Bubbles pop up with a giggly delight,
As all underwater join in the sight.
The ocean is laughing, a jovial spree,
With fish in tuxedos, it's quite a sight to see!

Colorful Choral Serenade

A parrotfish sings in colors so bright,
"Why do we swim? Well, it feels just right!"
With a splash and a flip, the group starts to sway,
In a disco of bubbles they dance and play!

The wrasses all gossip, with scales that shine,
"Did you hear what the puffer for dinner did dine?"
"Not a clue! But I hope it was snacks!" they cheer,
"Or maybe some plankton—oh, what a sheer!"

Anemones sway to the seaweed's soft beat,
"Let's throw a party, invite EVERYONE here!"
"Just don't let the eels come, they might bring the gloom,"

"But let's get the bass in, we need some real boom!"

With the sun shining through the blue water's veil,
They all swim together, a whimsical tale.
The laughs echo out, in a musical hush,
As creatures of all kinds join in the big rush!

Beneath the Waves, a Dialogue

"Hey, what's that? Oh wait, just a fish!"
The grouper exclaims with a goofy swish.
"I thought it was lunch, but look at it play!"
"Looks more like my cousin who's gone astray!"

The jellyfish floats, flickering bright,
"You guys are too dramatic, just chill out tonight!"
"Not all of us wiggle, some swim with style,"
"But the best part of swimming? The friends all the while!"

"What's that noise? Is it a whale?"
"No, just the currents, carrying tales.
Let's gather around, hear what they say,"
"Of the adventures we've had, and the games we play!"

The laughter resounds in the watery haze,
As the fish share their stories from sun-drenched days.
Beneath the vast blue, they all have their voice,
In this underwater realm, we all rejoice!

Echoes of the Tidal Realm

In the dance of the tides, a whisper rings true,
"What do you call sea creatures in a shoe?"
The fish all giggle, flopping around,
"Sole-mates, of course! Look, they're jelly-bound!"

The shrimp throw a roving disco beneath,
"Who's ready to party? Come join with no sheath!"
With bubbles and giggles, they boogie and sway,
"Life is too short, let's toast with some spray!"

"Did you hear the news? The murky eel's back!"
"Oh no! Beware of his treacherous snack!"
But they all start laughing, what a scene it could make,
The stories they tell as they wiggle and shake!

So in the deep waters where laughter sings loud,
Every scale, every fin, gathers in a crowd.
In echoes of joy that ripple through space,
The sea becomes home, a delightfully safe place!

Songs from the Silent Abyss

Underwater dances, fish in a line,
A crab wearing glasses, thinks he's divine.
The octopus juggles, with eight little hands,
Shouting out jokes to his jellyfish fans.

Seahorses tango, in twirls and in spins,
While starfish play poker, with shells on their chins.
Bubble-blowing turtles, all puffed up with pride,
Say 'What's that smell?' from a barnacle ride.

Clownfish are laughing, tickled by seaweed,
"Who knew we'd find humor, beneath the deep sea!"
While eels entertain, in their slinky ways,
Making fish giggle through bright ocean days.

So join in the giggles, as waves burst with cheer,
For every fish buddy, loves laughter and beer.
Under the surface, where the fun never ends,
There's always a party with gills as our friends.

Vibrations of the Vibrant Waters

Bubbles are bouncing, like popping balloons,
A dolphin crooning silly afternoon tunes.
The clownfish in stripes, say, 'We're fancy and bright!'
Doing the cha-cha, under disco light.

The hermit crabs groan, "We need better shells!"
As they swap 'em like hats, with hilarious yells.
A sea cucumber grins, says, 'I'm feeling quite flat,'
While oysters just chuckle, all snug in their chat.

Shrimps forming a band, with barnacles near,
Playing seaweed guitars, everyone cheers.
Anemones sway, to the rhythm below,
As fish do the limbo, just put on a show.

With laughter and splashes, the vibe's at its peak,
As underwater critters all dance to their beat.
In this watery world, where funny reigns high,
The spirit of joy will always apply.

Whispers of the Deep

The anglerfish whispers, with a light on his head,
'Who needs a match? I light up instead!'
The pufferfish giggles, puffing up with pride,
While a timid old crab tries to hide from the tide.

The swordfish is sharp, but has jokes up his sleeve,
'Why did the marlin never believe?'
The opinion of snails? Slow, but they say,
'We're keeping the gossip at bay every day!'

With dolphins who mime, making faces so cute,
And fluttering mantas, all dressed in a suit.
The laughter erupts as the sea horses play,
Creating a ruckus in their own special way.

As bubbles ascend, bursting into a whizz,
Creating a chorus of joys that just is.
In the quiet of depths, where the whispers are deep,
Every little creature has giggles to keep.

Echoes Beneath the Waves

Echoing laughter from a pirate fish crew,
Searching for treasure, with maps they drew.
The sea turtles chase, a wide sandy fleet,
While laughing seals play, mock 'Who's got more feet?'

Anemones brag, 'We've got the best threads!'
While wrasses share secrets, and giggle in beds.
The schooling fish dart, 'We're fast and we're sleek!'
'Headed to splash downs, just give us a peek!'

The conch shells are spinning, gossip swirling around,
With a mermaid chiming in, echoing sound.
Through currents they glide, with a chuckle and cheer,
In a bowl of the ocean, all laughter is clear.

So dive into humor, the deep has its charm,
In the echoes of fun, there's a sense of calm.
For amidst the tides, in the underwater craze,
The heart of the ocean echoes with plays.

Tides of Tranquility

The starfish do a dance, oh what a sight,
They twirl and they spin, in colored light.
The fish wear ties for their evening soiree,
While crabs play poker, what a silly play!

The seahorses giggle as they ride the waves,
Doing tricks and flips, just like little knaves.
A clam starts to sing, it's off-key but bold,
And all of the jellyfish laugh, uncontrolled!

The octopus juggles pearls with such flair,
While a group of small snails munch fun snacks to share.
The turtles host parties with bubbles so bright,
Making every fish dance, oh what pure delight!

So come take a dip in this water-filled glee,
Where laughter and joy sway like kelp in the sea.
With every splash and squeal, it's a circus set free,
In the tides of tranquility, endlessly!

Whispers in the Current

Underwater secrets, oh, who can hear?
A clam tells a tale filled with laughter and cheer.
The anemones chuckle as they sway to and fro,
While the shrimp tell tall tales of the crab's last show!

The eels make faces like they've lost their way,
With bubbles and giggles, they brighten the day.
A grouper named Gary, he's quite the sly fish,
He sneaks up on others, it's his favorite wish!

A turtle in shades, he's the king of the scene,
Claims he's got stories, though they're rarely seen.
Rays float on by, like they're in a parade,
Making each other laugh while they shimmy and sway!

So join in the fun, as we ride with the tide,
In the whispers of currents where chuckles reside.
Each coral a comedian, each fin a delight,
In this underwater realm, we soar like a kite!

Chorus of the Nautilus

A nautilus sings, with a voice like a charm,
While puffers puff up and try to stay calm.
The barnacles join, with their clappy old hands,
In this quirky sea concert, across the cool sands!

With a wink and a whirl, the fish drop their woes,
As dolphins do flips, and the seaweed just grows.
A crab with a kazoo leads the merry band,
While the whole ocean laughs in this joyful strand!

The starfish harmonize, with their five little arms,
As sea turtles groove, without any qualms.
Cuttlefish paint colors and dance on the stage,
Transforming the sea into a funny new page!

So let's join the chorus of creatures so bright,
Who sing through the currents, a true sea delight.
For in this sea symphony, laughter takes flight,
With the nautilus's songs that sparkle the night!

Dreaming in Seafoam

In seafoam dreams, where the laughter is light,
A fish with a top hat takes to the night.
He twirls with a wink, creating such glee,
While seahorses giggle, enjoying the spree!

The bubbles all float, like balloons in the air,
And mermaids join in for a whimsical fair.
Clams offer cupcakes, with frosting to spare,
While shrimps do a jig without any care!

The dolphins play catch with a shiny old shell,
And the sea cucumbers have stories to tell.
As the tide pulls us in, with a splash and a cheer,
We dance in the foam, with nothing to fear!

So let's dream in the waves, where the fun's always near,
In a world full of laughter, the oceans we cheer.
For in this seafoam, where the bright colors beam,
Life bubbles over, we're living the dream!

Beneath the Surface Secrets

In the ocean's depths, whispers float,
Clams gossip as they change their coat.
Starfish dance with a jellyfish's glow,
While seaweed sways to a crab's high show.

Seahorses giggle in a swirling twirl,
Eels in tuxedos, oh what a whirl!
A pufferfish shares a joke, quite round,
With a clownfish, laughter does abound.

Dolphins plot a prank on a lone shark,
While lobsters play tag till it gets dark.
Underwater tickles, bubbles arise,
The sea is a circus beneath sunny skies.

With seashells echoing tales of the deep,
Fish schools form laughter, no secrets to keep.
The ocean's a stage, and all play along,
Beneath the surface, the creatures sing strong.

The Language of the Fishes

Bubbles pop like laughter in the sea,
Fish chat in colors—just you and me.
A bass tells a bassoon joke so crude,
While a trumpet fish brings a good mood.

Tangs trade tales of adventures bold,
Each story brighter than the last told.
A grouper laughs at a newfangled fin,
While snappers giggle; it's a fishy din.

Blennies boast of their sandy homes,
While wrasses argue like old-time gnomes.
They swap their secrets and share their tricks,
With fins as fancy as circus flicks.

From tiny tetras to sleek barracuda,
There's humor aplenty, hidden and ruda.
They swim and they sparkle, with joy on their slates,
In this underwater kingdom, everyone relates.

Aquarelle of the Ocean

Dipped in hues of turquoise and gold,
The ocean's canvas, stories unfold.
Anemones dance with their frilly skirts,
While fish show off in their glittery shirts.

Giddy clownfish squeeze through bright corals,
Spreading laughter in tiny spirals.
With every brushstroke, they spin a tale,
In artistic strokes, they never fail.

Turtles glide with a graceful flair,
A sea lion pranks with a flipped-out hair.
The ocean's a palette, so vivid, so spry,
Painting joy where fishes leap and fly.

Glimmers and giggles swirl all around,
Each wave a punchline, a joyful sound.
In this watery art, life's a grand jest,
Doodle your dreams in the ocean's fest.

The Soundtrack of the Blue

In the deep blue sea, the music plays,
With bubbles and beats that brighten your days.
Octopus strums on a shell-cased drum,
While a parrotfish hums—a fishy strum.

Waves crash like cymbals, crashing and loud,
As sea turtles sway, so relaxed and proud.
The dolphins dance, a splashy ballet,
While stars twinkle softly, watching the play.

Seashells whisper tunes from times long past,
As the ocean's orchestra plays very fast.
The rhythm of currents, a soft melodious tease,
In the blue's sweet embrace, every fish aims to please.

Echos of laughter, like maracas shake,
Underwater grooving, for goodness' sake!
Join this concert, let your spirits lift,
The ocean's soundtrack is nature's best gift.

Symphony of Sunlit Depths

Bubbles rise like giggles in the sea,
Fish dance around with glee and spree.
A clownfish grins, what a joker,
Tickling the seaweed like a toker.

Seahorses waltz in pairs, so spry,
Gossiping shrimp wave hello, oh my!
Starfish share tales of their great escapes,
While crabs strut in their fancy capes.

The sea cucumbers quietly snicker,
Watching the turtles getting their vicker.
An octopus juggles with a sly smile,
Entertaining all in his stretchy style.

Underwater laughter fills the blue,
Even the sea urchins giggle too.
In this vibrant world full of cheer,
Nature's jesters always near.

Murmurs from the Abyss

Down below where light starts to fade,
Whispers of funny tales are made.
A grouper sings with a voice so deep,
Making the anglerfish lose his sleep.

Shrimps wear hats, in a funky duet,
Conducting a band with no fret or debt.
Their tiny sways bring giggles to all,
Even the whales can't help but sprawl.

The lobster tells jokes about his pincers,
While the small fish laugh, avoiding his winces.
Starry-eyed mackerels join in with flair,
Making a splash without a care.

Echoes of laughter in murky halls,
The deep-sea comedy never stalls.
With a wink and a twist, they play their part,
These garrulous creatures have sea-salt heart.

Lullabies for the Aquatic Realm

Turtles croon to the rhythm of waves,
Nudging the fish, all playful knaves.
A whale hums tunes, deep yet so sweet,
As dolphins flip in a bubbly treat.

Little clownfish join in, full of sass,
Making up stories with a splash and a dash.
The seaweed rustles, laughing along,
In this watery world, no need for a song.

With corals swaying to the giggly beats,
Even the anemones sway on their seats.
A pufferfish puffs up, all full of pride,
While a shy jellyfish tries to hide.

Giggling at night under the moon's glow,
The marine choir puts on quite a show.
Each note a sparkle in the dark, divine,
With laughter and joy, the sea feels fine.

The Tapestry of Marine Songs

Beneath the waves, where the colors collide,
Creatures gather, side by side.
A snapper cracks jokes, the gobby just grins,
While the wrasses chuckle, swimming in spins.

Anemones sway like they're part of a band,
Making the rhythm with their gentle hand.
Mackerel tease with their shimmering scales,
While eager squid share their comet trails.

The parrotfish chomps with a loud crunch,
With bubbles escaping in a silly bunch.
Lobsters tap dance on the sandy floor,
While the rascally shrimp yell, "Encore!"

In this sea of laughter, life's a delight,
Every creature joins in, both day and night.
From tiny plankton to mighty whale,
They weave their laughter, the ocean's tale.

Secrets of the Cerulean Realm

In the depths where fish do dance,
An octopus sneaks a sideways glance.
Clownfish juggling, what a sight!
A sea cucumber dreams of flight.

Starfish gossip, they're quite bold,
While sea urchins laugh, quite uncontrolled.
A whale hums tunes, low and sweet,
As a crab clicks claws in a funky beat.

Bright anemones sway with flair,
While a turtle combs his greasy hair.
A parrotfish munches like it's fine cuisine,
Dreaming of bubbles, sparkly and clean.

In the blue, oh what a show,
With fish in hats and eels in tow.
Join the fun, take a dive,
In this realm, we just thrive!

Melodies of Marine Life

A seahorse sings a chirpy tune,
While jellyfish float like balloons.
The dolphin squeaks with a splashy grin,
And a clam reveals her shiny chin.

Each wave a laugh, a ticklish tease,
As minnows dance through the swaying seas.
A flounder flops with comic flair,
And sea turtles learn to comb their hair.

Shrimps have disco parties, quite the scene,
With bubblegum popping, oh so keen.
The anglerfish tries to impress,
With a light-up dance, I must confess.

Dive in, let laughter be your guide,
Where every fin has fun and pride.
In every splash, hear joy's sweet chime,
As the ocean sings, it's party time!

Shimmering Tales of the Sea

A fish in sunglasses struts with flair,
While lobsters twirl without a care.
A hermit crab in a tiny shell,
Claims he's the king and dances well.

Bubble-blowing squids make quite a mess,
While turtles giggle, trying to impress.
Anemones wave, all in a rush,
As a fishy parade begins to crush.

The pufferfish jokes with a spiky grin,
Says, "Join my crew, we'll never fin!"
Mermaids chime in with laughter and song,
In these shimmering tales, you can't go wrong.

So dive beneath the sparkling blues,
With quirky friends, you cannot lose.
In the depths, joy swirls and plays,
Every moment's a splash of rays!

Rhythms of the Tides

The tides are grooving, can't you see?
With rhythm and blues from the fishy spree.
Octopuses twist in a swirling ballet,
While schools of fish dance hip-hop all day.

A crab on a rock sings out a tune,
To the rhythm of waves beneath the moon.
A dolphin flips, feeling the bass,
As seaweed sways, keeping up the pace.

A starfish claps its arms in delight,
While seagulls laugh, taking flight.
The ocean's symphony fills the air,
With quirky creatures, singing everywhere.

So come and sway, lose all your cares,
Join the marine, without any snares.
In the blue, fun never subsides,
These are the joyful rhythms of tides!

Cradle of the Sea Creatures

In the water, fish dance with glee,
A crab wears a hat, thinking he's free.
Seahorses prance in their tiny parade,
While clams giggle softly, all quite unafraid.

The octopus plays a tricky old game,
He changes his colors but still feels the same.
With a wink and a swirl, he steals the scene,
As snails take a selfie, feeling quite keen.

The jellyfish floats like a balloon,
Bouncing along to a quirky tune.
Starfish strike poses, they're quite the show,
"I'm so great," they boast, "just thought you should know!"

Down in this haven of wobbly fun,
Every critter knows why it's second to none.
They dance and they laugh, in a swirling delight,
Under the waves, where the sun is just right.

Reflections of a Fathoms' Depth

The deep sea whispers secrets and dreams,
Where fish tell tall tales with outrageous themes.
Anemones giggle at the sight of a clown,
While sea turtles glide, looking royal and brown.

The depth holds a party that's quite offbeat,
Where a shrimp dresses up in a flashy new seat.
"Look at me shine!" says a pufferfish bold,
While octos can't stop the stories they've told.

From mollusks' corners, there's chatter so slick,
About a fish that swam fast, but was really quite thick.
A squid tells a tale from a book of surprise,
With ink-splattered pages beneath the blue skies.

As bubbles rise up like laughter and cheer,
The depth of the ocean is where we adhere.
Living in water, so silly and bright,
Bringing us joy under moonlight's sweet light.

Kaleidoscope of the Ocean's Heart

A parrotfish munches on colorful snacks,
While a playful sea otter shows off his hacks.
The clownfish chuckle, they're quite the jesters,
Bouncing around like proper fun investors.

Electric eels hum a jazzy old tune,
As crabs play the drums with shells as their boon.
A dolphin does flips, with so much finesse,
Squeaking and squealing, they always impress.

The hermit crab flaunts a jewel of a shell,
While tiny fish gossip on who's not so swell.
Surrounded by colors that shift and that swirl,
It's a dazzling dance in this underwater world.

Through seaweed jungles where laughter is found,
Whimsical creatures spin round and round.
In this vibrant land, where joy plays its part,
Lives a whimsical dream of the ocean's own heart.

Nautical Narratives

The sunken ship tells tales of old,
Of kraken encounters and treasures untold.
A mermaid laughs, brushing her long hair,
While fish weave a story, quite light as air.

The seashells gossip, oh what a sound,
As starfish engage in a roundabout round.
"We saw a whale that wore a tall hat,
And danced in the waves—imagine that!"

Eel whispers secrets from caves down below,
As fish play charades, each putting on a show.
In this underwater saga, a grand masquerade,
Where everyone giggles in the soft, swaying jade.

With each passing tide, new stories arise,
From dolphins to plankton, all under our skies.
These nautical narratives brightly unfold,
In the laughter of waves, forever retold.

In the Embrace of Currents

Fish in bow ties swim with glee,
Jellyfish dancing, oh what a spree!
Starfish clapping, they're quite the band,
While crabs juggle seashells on the sand.

Octopus throws a wild costume ball,
Anemones giggle, they're having a ball!
With each wave, laughter fills the sea,
Bubbles whisper jokes, oh can't you see?

Seahorses twirl in a waltz so fine,
Dolphins leap, they're doing just fine!
A clownfish jokes, "Life's a grand jest!"
Under the waves, they love their quest.

So come aboard this whimsical ride,
Join the fish in the ocean's tide!
Laughter echoes through the bright blue,
In this undersea world, fun's never through!

Sea Shanties in Stillness

A lobster sings a sea shanty bold,
With a voice that warms like tales of old.
The seagulls join in, creating a choir,
As waves caper, they never tire.

Crabs tap dance, their claws like castanets,
While fish share secrets, no one forgets.
With shells for drums, they keep up the beat,
Bubbles of laughter make life so sweet.

Turtles tell tales of their ancient dread,
While sea cucumbers nod their green head.
In the calm of the sea, joy's on parade,
With every splash, a sweet serenade.

Together they sing till the moon says goodbye,
Waving their fins as the stars fill the sky.
In the ocean's embrace, their spirits ignite,
Echoes of mirth, in the soft, silver light.

Undersea Echoes of Time

A sponge wears glasses, reading a book,
  While fishes gossip, oh what a nook!
Seashells compose, in tunes they delight,
  Echoes of laughter fill the deep night.

A pufferfish blows up, it's a funny sight,
While turtles in crowns revel in the light.
Squids share puns, ink spills with joy,
  Creating murals, a colorful ploy.

Angelfish giggle, as they dance and sway,
  Reminding the ocean that it's a fun day!
With every current, the jokes cascade,
And a sea serpent joins in, don't be afraid!

Between the corals, whispers of cheer,
In this watery world, there's nothing to fear.
So swim along, where the giggles resound,
In the heart of the ocean, where joy is found!

The Realm of Marine Reverie

In a realm where sea stars spin and glide,
The funny fish frolic, no need to hide.
With a wink and a splash, they dance around,
Creating ripples of laughter—joy unbound.

Hermit crabs race, it's the highlight of the day,
While echinoderms cheer from the rocky ballet.
With seaweed confetti, they celebrate life,
In this jovial sphere, there's never strife.

The sea otters juggle pearls with flair,
While a nearby clam offers a silly stare.
With bubbles like balloons, they rise with glee,
In the kingdom of fun, just wait and see!

So dive right in, and let your heart sing,
Join the merry crew, where joy is king.
In the depths of the blue, where laughter's the game,
Every splash is a giggle, forever the same!

Sonnet of the Sea Creatures

In a world where the fish like to prance,
A clownfish in stripes, always ready to dance.
The starfish just laughs as he sticks to his rock,
Says, "Look at my moves, oh, you fish in the flock!"

The octopus juggles with shells on a spree,
While dolphins pass by, giggling full of glee.
"Did you hear about Shark?" one angelfish quips,
"He tried to do ballet, and I swear he flips!"

A seahorse told tales of a lost treasure chest,
But when they dove down, they found only a vest.
The pufferfish puffed, with a grin so wide,
"I'd wear that old thing! Just don't let me glide!"

In this ocean of laughter, the waves seem to sing,
With bubbles that giggle, and jellies that swing.
So let's raise our shells for a toast to the sea,
Where every fish whispers, "Join in the spree!"

Harmonies of the Underwater Garden

In the garden below where the fishes reside,
Anemones gossip while crabs scuttle wide.
"I've got the best jokes, just listen and see!"
The pufferfish chuckled, floating carefree.

A turtle named Ted wore a hat from a clam,
"I'm the stylish one here, just call me your fam!"
While sea cucumbers rolled, all covered in green,
"Fashion's a whirlpool, we're trendy, I mean!"

Blowfish blow kisses, but be careful they're spikey,
While plankton dance round, their vibe ever likey.
The seahorses sway, like they're in a grand ball,
"Step right up, don't be shy, come twirl with us all!"

Cocoa the clownfish taught all how to joke,
"Why did the crab never share? It's a hoax!"
With laughter and bubbles, the sea life would cheer,
In this vibrant garden, there's always good cheer!

Conversations in the Currents

Deep down in the currents, where fish love to chat,
A grouper named Gary wore quite a tall hat.
"I'm going to the ball, it's a grand fishy tease!"
While the shrimp on the side cracked jokes, "Bring the cheese!"

The lionfish pranced with a look quite so grand,
"I'm the king of the sea, with my poisonous brand!"
The parrotfish laughed, "You can't scare a spout!
With colors so bright, who could ever doubt?"

A turtle chimed in, "Now hear me, my friends,
What's the best ocean drink? A sea-weed amends!"
They chuckled and chortled, in bubbles of bliss,
"Oh, what fun it is, to share moments like this!"

With seashells for microphones, laughter would flow,
Every wave a punchline, a perfect sea show.
As the currents carried their hilarious tales,
The ocean, a canvas, where joy never fails!

The Language of Gills and Fins

In waters so blue, the fish talk in style,
Bubbles bursting forth, they share jokes with a smile.
"Did you hear the one about the fish with a cold?
He said, 'I'm not fine, I'm just feeling quite old!'"

The crabs clicked their claws, adding puns to the scene,
While seahorses twirled, looking quite like a queen.
"Why did the starfish go party all night?
He finally found shells that were just out of sight!"

The jellyfish floated, with grace and with flair,
"Being translucent is hard, but who needs a hair?
Just look at my glow, like a lamp, I'm divine!
In the depths of the sea, we shine, that's our line!"

So they laughed, the sea creatures, with fins intertwined,
Learning that joy is a treasure we find.
In the depths of the ocean, their laughter would ring,
In a language that only brave fish ever bring!

Secrets of the Seafloor

Bubbles laugh and swim about,
Fish in wigs, they scream and shout.
Anemones juggle seashells bright,
Underwater parties last all night.

Crabs in sunglasses dance and twirl,
While clams gossip, pearls they unfurl.
Sea turtles wear bow ties and cheer,
Tickled by the ocean's salty sphere.

Starfish play cards, with fins so sly,
Eels attempt a stand-up high.
Seahorses ride bikes racing fast,
Chasing the current, fun unsurpassed.

Lobsters mime, strut like they're bold,
With tales of treasure that should be told.
The seafloor's secrets outshine the rest,
In this kingdom of laughter, we are truly blessed.

Beneath the Waves' Embrace

In the depths where the sillies tread,
Octopuses tell tales from their bed.
Grouper in pajamas, how they sway,
Breaking out in dance, come join the fray!

Jellyfish bounce like jellybeans,
While damsels trade their silly means.
Fish with fedoras nod their best,
Sardines sardine together, quite a fest.

A grumpy goatfish zips around,
With flippers waving, makes a sound.
Underwater puns swim with glee,
Tickling the fins of giddy sea debris.

While sea cucumbers snack all day,
Puffers puff up, they join the play.
Beneath the waves where laughter swims,
Mirth and magic drip like gems.

The Dreamers of the Deep

In the realm where the dreamers dive,
Clownfish laugh, oh, how they thrive!
With bubbles forming silly shapes,
They hatch their plans like ocean grapes.

The anglerfish, with a lantern bright,
Wants to shine like a star on sight.
But in its glow, a shrimp appears,
Singing jigs to dispel its fears.

A sea horse prances all around,
While narwhals play tag, oh what a sound!
With a flick of their tails and a splash,
Creating waves that make all dash.

As dolphins break into comic skits,
The sea life roars with joyful bits.
In the blue abyss, they jest and beam,
Together they weave the brightest dream.

Sonnet of the Sailfin

Oh, sailfin fish, with style and flair,
You twirl through currents with grace so rare.
With fins that flutter like banners bright,
In playful displays, oh what a sight!

They bob and weave, like dancers in sync,
Switching their colors, oh how they think!
While parrotfish chatter in secret tones,
Making puns that ripple through ocean zones.

The wiggly worms join in the fun,
While the seahorses take a quick run.
In underwater caverns where mirth prevails,
Laughter erupts as the fun never fails.

So here's to the sailors of finned delight,
Making every dive a whimsical flight!

www.ingramcontent.com/pod-product-compliance
Lightning Source LLC
Chambersburg PA
CBHW070005300426
43661CB00141B/227